13

The Old Lift

by Alison Hawes

Illustrated by Aleksandar Sotirovski

Titles in Ignite

Alien Sports TV	Jonny Zucker
Monster Diner	Danny Pearson
Team Games	Melanie Joyce
Mutant Baby Werewolf	Richard Taylor
Rocket Dog	Lynda Gore
The Old Lift	Alison Hawes
Spiders from Space	Stan Cullimore
Gone Viral	Mike Gould
The Ghost Train	Roger Hurn
Dog Diaries	Clare Lawrence

Badger Publishing Limited
Suite G08, Stevenage,
Hertfordshire SG1 2DX
Telephone: 01438 791037   Fax: 01438 791036
www.badgerlearning.co.uk

The Old Lift ISBN 978-1-84926-961-2

Publisher: Susan Ross
Senior Editor: Danny Pearson
Designer: Fiona Grant
Illustrator: Aleksandar Sotirovski

The Old Lift

Contents

Vocabulary:

grabbed   emergency

spooky   corridor

flickered   ambulance

Main characters:

Mick

Jen

Gran

Chapter 1
Blackout

Mick and Jen were walking to Gran's.

Suddenly, the sky went dark and
it began to rain.

Mick grabbed his sister's arm. "Come
on, Jen!" he yelled. "I'm getting wet!"

There was a big flash of lightning and
a clap of thunder. Jen hated thunder
and lightning.

They ran down the road to the old
block of flats. Gran's flat was on the
top floor.

There was a big flash of lightning.
It lit up the dark block of flats.

"Spooky!" Mick laughed.

"Stop it!" said Jen. "That's not funny."

They ran inside, out of the storm.
Mick pressed the lift button. The doors
opened and Mick got in.

"I'm going to walk up the stairs," said
Jen. "I hate that lift. It's old and
creaky!"

But there was another big clap of
thunder. It made Jen jump.

Mick laughed as she ran into the lift, after all. The lift doors closed.

The lights in the lift flickered off and on.

"Spooky!" laughed Mick.

"Stop it!" yelled Jen. "I told you. That's not funny!"

But then, all the lights went out and the lift stopped. Inside the lift, it was pitch black.

Mick stopped laughing.

"What shall we do?" wailed Jen.

"Don't panic!" Mick said, "I'll phone Gran."

Mick pulled his mobile out of his pocket. Jen could see his face in the light from his phone.

"What's the matter?" she asked.

"I don't know what to do," he wailed. "There's no signal. The phone's dead!"

Chapter 2

Never again!

"Give me the phone," said Jen.

"I told you. There's no signal," said Mick.

"I know," she said, "but I need the light to find something."

Jen shone the light around the lift. "There it is!" she said.

In the dim light from the phone, she read a notice.

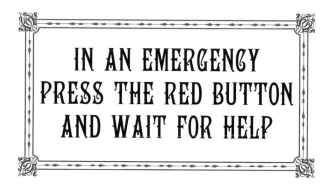

IN AN EMERGENCY
PRESS THE RED BUTTON
AND WAIT FOR HELP

The red button was high up on the lift wall.

"I'll get it," said Mick.

But before he could press the button, the lights came back on. The lift jumped into life.

"That's the last time I go in there," said Jen as they reached the top floor.

"Yes, never again!" said Mick.
Mick rang the bell to Gran's flat.

"Come in. It's not locked," said Gran.

Gran was sitting on her chair. Her right foot was in plaster. Her dog, Sniffer, was lying at her feet.

Mick and Jen sat down and told Gran about the lift.

As they talked, the lights in her flat flickered off and on. Sniffer began to howl.

"Be quiet, Sniffer," said Gran.

Down the corridor, a door slammed.

Some people were shouting.

Sniffer raced to the door. He began barking and scratching at the door.

"What's the matter with Sniffer?" asked Jen.

"I don't know," said Gran. "He's been acting oddly all day."

Chapter 3

In danger

"I expect Sniffer just wants a walk," said Jen.

"Come on, then," said Mick. "It's stopped raining. We can take him out now."

"Thanks," said Gran, "but don't go in that lift."

"No way!" laughed Jen.

But when they went out the door, Sniffer ran down the corridor to the lift.

"Come back!" called Jen.

But Sniffer took no notice and ran into the open lift.

"Oh no!" said Jen.

"Don't panic," laughed Mick, "Sniffer can't press the lift buttons!"

As they walked down the corridor, they could hear shouting again. It was coming from the flat by the lift.

A woman came out of the flat. She looked upset. She pushed past Mick and Jen, as though she hadn't seen them.

She got into the lift and closed the doors.

Mick ran to the lift and banged on the doors. "Wait!" he shouted.

But it was no good. The lift was on its way down. Mick and Jen could hear Sniffer barking.

They ran back down the corridor and down the stairs. But something was wrong! The lift was going too fast.

Mick and Jen stared in horror as the lift hurtled down the lift shaft.

Chapter 4

Trapped!

There was the sound of metal scraping against metal. There was a shower of sparks. Then the lift suddenly slowed and screeched to a stop at the ground floor.

Mick and Jen ran to the bottom of the stairs.

The caretaker came out of his flat as Mick and Jen ran past. "What's going on?" he yelled.

"The lift has crashed," Mick said. "There's a dog and a woman inside!"

Mick shouted at the woman through the lift door. "Are you okay in there?" he said.

But there was no answer. All they could hear was Sniffer whimpering and scratching at the door to get out.

Mick shouted again. "Are you OK in there?"

But still there was no answer. "Quick! We must get her out!" said Jen. "She must be badly hurt!"

Jen pressed and pressed the lift button. But nothing happened.

Mick and the caretaker tried to pull the doors apart. But it was no good. They wouldn't open.

The dog and the woman were trapped!

The caretaker phoned for the fire brigade and ambulance.

"Help is on its way!" Mick shouted through the lift door.

But still there was no reply.

It took half an hour, but the firemen got the doors open in the end. Sniffer rushed out and Mick and Jen hugged him tight.

"I thought you said, there was a woman in here?" said an ambulance man.

"Yes," said Mick.

"So, where is she?" he said, angrily.

Jen and Mick looked into the lift.

It was empty!

Chapter 5

The accident

"We don't like people who make things up," said the ambulance man.

"But she has to be there!" said Mick. "We saw her get into the lift."

"She got in on the top floor," said Jen. "She came out of the flat by the lift."

"Now I know you're making things up!" said the caretaker. "That flat is empty. No one has lived in it for years."

"But we're not making it up!" Mick shouted. "We did see her!"

"We heard a man and a woman shouting," said Jen. "And we saw a light on in the flat."

The caretaker pulled his keys out of his pocket. "Come on," he said, "I'm going to show you that flat is empty."

They climbed back to the top floor. Sniffer ran ahead. He scratched at the door of the flat by the lift.

The door swung open.

"See!" said Mick. "We told you there was someone in the flat."

But inside, the flat was cold and dark and empty.

Mick tried the light switch. But nothing happened.

"See!" said the caretaker. "I told you. No-one lives here."

"But I don't understand," said Mick,
"We did see her!"

"Perhaps you saw a ghost," laughed
the caretaker.

Sniffer began to howl.

"I don't like it in here," wailed Jen.
"I want to see my Gran."

Chapter 6

The photo

Mick and Jen told Gran about the lady in the lift. Gran's face went as white as a sheet.

"What's the matter?" asked Jen.

"Two people lived in that flat ten years ago," said Gran. "The woman was killed in an accident."

"Her husband never got over it," she went on. "He moved out a few weeks later. He died the same year."

"But what's that got to do with the woman we saw today?" asked Jen.

"Pass me that scrapbook," said Gran, "and I'll show you."

Jen took a book down from the shelf and handed it to Gran.

Gran turned the pages. "Here it is," she said. "I cut it out of the paper."

Gran began to read.

Woman killed in accident

On May the 6th, a woman was killed in an accident.

She was named as Mary West, of 5A, Dunsford Flats. Her husband, Gary, said they had had a silly row.

He said his wife had been upset when she got in the lift to go to the shops.

The driver of the lorry that hit her said, "She stepped right out in front of me. There was nothing I could do."

"Look at the date," said Gran, turning the book, towards the children.

"The accident happened on the 6th of May. It's the 6th of May today."

"That's spooky!" said Mick. Then Mick looked at Jen. She was shaking.

"What's the matter?" Mick asked.

"Look at the photo!" she said.

Mick looked at the photo.

"That's the woman we saw today," Jen said.

"That's really spooky!" said Mick.

But he wasn't laughing.

The Tower of London

The Tower of London

Is the Tower of London haunted?

Some people think so.
They say there are many ghosts.

Many people were kept prisoner here.
Many were tortured.
Many were put to death.

It is said that many of those who died haunt the Tower today.

The ghost of the White Lady sometimes walks in the White Tower. Some say they can smell her perfume.

The ghost of King Henry VI is said to haunt the Wakefield Tower. He was stabbed to death there in 1471.

Some people say they have seen the ghosts of two young princes in the Bloody Tower.

A ghostly monk is said to haunt Traitors' Gate.

Questions

Where were Mick and Jen going and what was Jen scared of?

What did the notice in the lift say?

Why could Gran not take Sniffer for a walk?

Who did the caretaker phone for help?

Why was the ambulance man cross with Mick and Jen?

Why was the caretaker sure Mick and Jen were making things up?

What was it like inside the flat by the lift?

What does, Gran's face went as white as a sheet mean?

What made Mick and Jen believe they had seen a ghost?